The Aquinas Lecture, 1960

LANGUAGE, TRUTH AND POETRY

Under the Auspices of the Aristotelian Society
of Marquette University

by
VICTOR M. HAMM, Ph.D.

MARQUETTE UNIVERSITY PRESS
MILWAUKEE
1960

Library of Congress Catalogue Card Number: 60-9736

© COPYRIGHT 1960
BY THE ARISTOTELIAN SOCIETY
OF MARQUETTE UNIVERSITY

PRINTED
IN
U.S.A.

Prefatory

The Aristotelian Society of Marquette University each year invites a scholar to deliver a lecture in honor of St. Thomas Aquinas. Customarily delivered on a Sunday close to March 7, the feast day of the society's patron saint, the lectures are called the Aquinas lectures.

In 1960 the Aquinas lecture "Language, Truth and Poetry" was delivered on March 6 in the Peter A. Brooks Memorial Union of Marquette University by Dr. Victor M. Hamm, professor of English, Marquette University.

Dr. Hamm was born in Milwaukee, Wisconsin on February 21, 1904. He received his A.B. degree from Marquette in 1926 and his M.A. degree in 1928. In 1929 he received a second M.A. degree from Harvard University followed by the awarding of the Ph.D. degree from Harvard in 1932.

During 1932 and 1933 Dr. Hamm travelled through England, France, and Italy as a Sheldon Travelling Scholar from Harvard. Following his return he accepted a position as instructor in English at St. Louis University and remained there until 1934. From 1934 to 1937 he was assistant professor of English at the College of Mount St. Joseph, Cincinnati, Ohio.

In 1937 he returned to Marquette as associate professor of English and in 1945 was promoted to professor. Dr. Hamm was named visiting professor at the University of Freiburg, Germany in 1952, and in 1957 he held the same position at the University of Wisconsin.

His published books and monographs include a translation with an introduction to *Pico Della Mirandola*: *Of Being and Unity* (Milwaukee: Marquette University Press, 1942); *The Pattern of Criticism* (Milwaukee: Bruce, 1951); and *The College Book of English Literature*, a joint effort with J. E. Tobin and William Hines (New York: American Book Co., 1949).

Another monograph, *Taste and the Audio-Visual Arts*, was published by the Marquette University Press on February 1, 1960.

In addition, Dr. Hamm has contributed articles to *Thought*, *The New Scholasticism*, *PMLA*, *Philological Quarterly*, *Journal of Aesthetics*, and *Comparative Literature*.

To his writings the Aristotelian Society has the pleasure of adding *Language, Truth and Poetry*.

Language, Truth
and
Poetry

Much has been written about the nature
of language and the nature of poetry, the
relation of language to poetry, and of
poetry to truth. With the pullulation of
philosophies and theories of language and
of poetry which have marked our day we
have landed in what looks like a real mare's
nest of opinion and speculation. Never,
apparently, was confusion worse con-
founded. Never was it more difficult to
find one's way about in the maze of ide-
ologies and theories. Bibliographies ac-
cumulate; controversies rage. One seems
to be standing on one of the uncompleted
tiers of the Tower of Babel after the confusion of tongues. This may, indeed, be
only the illusion of the ignoramus lost in

the maze of learning, but it is a real predicament for the ignoramus just the same. I am that ignoramus, and if Socrates was right in his conviction that his only claim to superiority above other men lay in his consciousness of the fact that he knew nothing, that proud assertion of intellectual humility might be my consolation. But Socrates was too humble—or too proud! We can, after all, know something in our human way of knowing, which is tentative and shadowy, but not, I think, illusory. If we have not the intellects of angels, neither are we condemned to the dark subrational gropings of the beast. If knowledge is difficult, it is not impossible.

With these preliminaries disposed of, I shall try to examine the state of affairs as I see it in the area my title suggests, paying particular attention to two extreme views of the problem of language, truth, and poetry, and attempting a third view which may, I hope, commend itself more to our sense of reality.

I.

We are still living intellectually—despite recent developments away from its crude original form—in the atmosphere of positivism, for perhaps the reigning school of philosophy in Great Britain and the United States is that of Logical Positivism deriving from the Cambridge School of Analysis and the Vienna Circle.[1] These philosophers are particularly concerned with language; in fact, they conceive of philosophy as nothing more than logical analysis, *i.e.*, as a clarification of the language of everyday. Let us look briefly at Professor A. J. Ayer's *Language, Truth,*

[1] Cf. Gustav Bergmann, *The Metaphysics of Logical Positivism*, (New York: Longmans, Green, 1954); John A. Dineen, "The Course of Logical Positivism," in *The Modern Schoolman*, XXXIV (1957), 1-21. For the "recent developments" alluded to in my text, cf. A. J. Ayer, W. C. Kneale, *et al.*, *The Revolution in Philosophy* (New York: St. Martin's Press, 1956), and Father Francis C. Wade's review of this book in *The New Scholasticism*, XXXII (1958), 121-23.

and Logic, from the title of which book I have taken the cue for my present lecture. This book, first published at London in 1936, has, says Gustav Bergmann in his examination of the school, attained almost the status of a text-book.[2] A sampling of Professor Ayer's positions as expressed in key statements throughout this little volume will indicate what the logical positivist thinks of language, and what hope for truth and for poetry exists on this foundation.[3]

Ayer's view of philosophy as mere linguistic analysis leads him to deny to propositions any validity other than tautology or empirical verifiability. Thus:

To say that a proposition is true is just to assert it, and to say that it is false is just to assert its contradictory. And this indicates that the terms 'true' and 'false' connote nothing, but function in the

[2] *Op. cit.,* p. 35.
[3] My references are to the revised edition of Ayer's book (London: Victor Gollancz, 1949).

sentence simply as marks of assertion and denial. . . . The traditional conception of truth as a 'real quality' or a 'real relation' is due . . . to a failure to analyse sentences correctly.[4]

Fundamental ethical concepts are more pseudoconcepts. . . . Sentences which simply express moral judgments do not say anything.[5]

Aesthetic terms are used in exactly the same way as ethical terms. Such aesthetic words as 'beautiful' and 'hideous' are employed, as ethical words are employed, not to make statements of fact, but simply to express certain feelings and evoke a certain response. . . . The critic, by calling attention to certain features of the work under review, and expressing his own feelings about them, endeavours to make us share his attitude towards the work as a whole.[6]

[4] *Ibid.*, pp. 88-89.
[5] *Ibid.*, pp. 107-108.
[6] *Ibid.*, pp. 113-114.

All metaphysical utterances are meaning-less.[7] And so on.

I am not going to enter on a critique of Professor Ayer or of the Logical Positivism he represents. Even if I were equal to this task, it would transcend the area of the present lecture. I am interested here only in what becomes of poetry on the premises of this school of linguistic analysis. Let me say, however, that the mind that can construct the system of Logical Positivism cannot itself be limited by the tenets of that philosophy, for in order to establish limits one must transcend those very limits. The propositions of Logical Positivism are therefore themselves metaphysical: they assert the reality of language, if nothing else.

It is instructive to note that in Ayer's book from which I have been quoting there is only a single reference to the

[7] *Ibid.*, cf. Chapter I: "The Elimination of Metaphysics."

poet; he is described as "the man who uses language emotively."[8] The man who uses language scientifically, according to Ayer, "is primarily concerned with the expression of true propositions," the poet, on the other hand, "with the creation of a work of art." But "a work of art" is comprised of propositions all of which are "literally false." On the terms of this school, therefore, poetry as a cognitive transaction becomes impossible, all that remains of it being, as the early I. A. Richards put it, "emotive utterance" and "pseudostatement."[9] What has happened in this aesthetic is that "poetry has simply fallen out of it, and it has become one stimulus among many which can produce desirable results"[10]—like a drink of bourbon,

[8] *Ibid.*, pp. 44-45.
[9] *Principles of Literary Criticism* (New York: Harcourt, Brace & Co., 1924), pp. 261 ff.
[10] D. G. James, *Scepticism and Poetry* (London: G. Allen & Unwin, 1937), p. 57. James further points out (p. 71) that Richards "has failed to see that the 'world-picture of science' is an

for example, or the feel of velvet. Hence critics with any conviction of the value of poetry as cognitive expression have opposed this view with might and main. John Crowe Ransom, for example, has pointed out that if emotional response is all that a poem is able to produce, then the labor of the poet in putting the poem into a particular shape of linguistic organization is vain.[11] And Mr. Allen Tate more conclusively attacks the positivist position in

imaginative construction, evolved with a view to the formulation of generalizations of strictest fact. He therefore takes it seriously for an account of the nature of existence. In his psychology, materialistic associationism accordingly becomes inevitable, the mind becomes for him the nervous system, and it is indifferent to him whether or not we call awareness a mental or a neural event."

[11] *The New Criticism* (New York: New Directions, 1941), pp. 32 ff. Cf. also: Stanley E. Hyman, *The Armed Vision: A Study in the Methods of Modern Literary Criticism* (New York: A. A. Knopf, 1948), Chap. 9; Wm. K. Wimsatt, Jr., and Cleanth Brooks, *Literary Criticism: A Short History* (New York: A. A. Knopf, 1957), Chaps. 27 and 28.

his essay "Literature as Knowledge," in which he draws the just conclusion that "since the language of poetry can be shown to be not strictly relevant to object-situations as these are presented by the positivist techniques, poetry becomes either nonsense or hortatory rhctoric."[12] The world of positivism, he says, "is a world without minds to know the world."[13] And, taking his cue from the later Richards, who himself had repudiated the positivist position, he elaborates the latter's description of poetry as "the completest mode of utterance," as follows:

The mode of completeness that it [poetry] achieves in the great works of the imagination is not the order of expcrimental completeness aimed at by the positivist sciences, whose responsibility is directed toward the verification of limited techniques. The completeness

[12] "Literature as Knowledge," in *The Man of Letters in the Modern World* (New York: Meridian Books, 1955), p. 50.
[13] *Ibid.*, p. 62.

of science is an abstraction covering an ideal of cooperation among specialized methods. No one can have an experience of sciences, or of a single science. For the completeness of *Hamlet* is not of the experimental order, but of the experienced order; it is, in short, of the mythical order.[14]

And this brings me to the other chief contemporary approach to language and poetry, the way of myth, to which I shall give more extended consideration, since it is a much more fruitful and widely exploited approach to our subject.

II.

If the Logical Positivists have tried to turn language into a kind of algebra, with nothing but univocal denotations adhering to the word-signs, the "Mythologists"—to call them that—actually assimilate language to myth, and myth to poetry. Thus a recent writer representing this attitude:

[14] *Ibid.,* pp. 62-3.

We can, I suggest, find means in the study of media as languages, and languages as myths. . . . Languages old and new, as macromyths, have their relation to words and word-making that characterizes the fullest scope of myth.[15]

So also Paul Valéry: "Myth is the name for everything that exists and subsists only on the basis of language."[16] Language is myth. Myth is poetry. "The word 'myth,'" writes Richard Chase, summing up a whole book on the subject, "means story: a myth is a tale, a narrative, or a poem; myth is literature and must be considered as an aesthetic creation of the human imagination."[17] This is all quite different from

[15] Marshall McLuhan, "Myth and Mass Media, in *Daedalus: Journal of the American Academy of Arts and Sciences*, LXXXVIII (1959), pp. 348, 340.

[16] "On Myths and Mythology" in *Paul Valéry: Selected Writings* (New York: New Directions, 1950), p. 199.

[17] *The Quest for Myth* (Baton Rouge: Louisiana State University Press, 1949), p. 73. This is in many respects a brilliant book, covering

Logical Positivism, as we shall see more clearly in a moment.

It is worth noting the historical fact that both the foundations of modern positivism and the reaction to it belong to the same century, the eighteenth. David Hume and Jeremy Bentham dehydrated language and reduced the mind, which is the organ of language, to a calculating machine. These were the forerunners of our Logical Positivists. But even before

the history of attitudes toward and theories of myth from Plato to the present. Its deeper thesis is apparent from the following excerpts: "The tensions aroused and the reconciliations affected between the religious desire for an omnipotent deity and the general human preference for powerful anthropomorphic and theriomorphic beings are universally stamped on mythology." (p. 84). "I suggest that myth dramatizes in poetic form the disharmonies, the deep neurotic disturbances which may be occasioned by this clash of inward and outward forces, and that by reconciling the opposing forces, by making them interact coercively toward a common end, myth performs a profoundly beneficial and life-giving act." (p. 85).

they had begun to write (indeed, before Bentham himself was born), the Italian Giambattista Vico, whose *Scienza Nuova* (1725) had to wait until our day to assert its influence and win its proper acclaim, elaborated the theory of myth as a kind of poetic language, the only language of which man was capable in the primitive stage of his development. Vico had been thinking of the past; for him the primitive age was over and done. But his theory was soon to be applied to poetry here and now. Later in the same century the German J. G. Herder "boldly derived language from the mythic process and made the special character of poetry reside in the fact that poetry preserves the dynamic quality of myth."[18] Herder was the true

[18] Wimsatt and Brooks, *op. cit.*, p. 700. Man, according to Herder *(Über den Ursprung der Sprache)*, invented language "from the tones of living nature, and made them signs of his growing reason." The origins of poetry and language are for Herder the same. Cf. also R. Welleck, *A History of Modern Criticism*

founder of the antirationalistic, romantic philology which lies at the root of the views and theories of the Mythologists. We are face to face here with a phenomenon all-embracing in its scope, to which the name "primitivism" has been given. It ramifies into history, politics, criticism, philosophy, the arts, even theology. "Back to Nature!"—"The man who thinks is a depraved animal" (Rousseau)—"The Specter is the Reasoning Power in Man" (Blake)—such were the slogans which epitomized while they signalized the overthrow of rationalism and the advent of unreason.

What did this mean for language, for poetry and the "truth" of poetry? For language it meant turning to the dynamics of speech and relating these, in turn, to the dynamics of sensation and feeling, for in these lay the true foundation, "the origi-

(2 vols.; New Haven: Yale University Press, 1955), I, 187.

nal creative potency of spiritual life."[19]
"With me," said the German Johann Georg
Hamann, *language* is the mother of reason and revelation, the Alpha and Ome-
ga."[20] Language seems here indeed to pre-
cede consciousness. One gets the same
thing in the English Romantics. "The
doctrine that words create knowledge," in
the language of a recent study, "is part
of the romantic theory of the imagination.
Coleridge, for example, constantly verges
upon such a conception."[21] "Are not
words," Coleridge asks in a letter to William Godwin, "parts and germinations of
the plant? And what is the law of their
growth? In something of this sort I would
endeavour to destroy the old antithesis of
Words and Things, elevating, as it were,

---

[19] Cf. Ernst Cassirer, *The Philosophy of Symbolic
Forms*, trans. Ralph Manheim (New Haven:
Yale University Press, 1953), I (*Language*),
150. A magisterial study.
[20] *Briefwechsel mit Jacobi*, ed. Gildemeister
(Gotha, 1868), p. 122.
[21] Wimsatt and Brooks, *op. cit.*, p. 584.

Words into things and living things too."[22]

For poetry it meant a similar creative prerogative. Shelley sums up the romantic apotheosis of the poet:

> Poets are not only *the authors of language* and of music, of the dance, and architecture, and statuary, and painting; they are the institutors of laws, and the founders of civil society, and the inventors of the arts of life, and the teachers, who draw into a certain propinquity with the beautiful and the true, that partial apprehension of the agencies of the invisible world which is called religion.[23]

This, and more, they accomplish, according to Shelley, in virtue of their faculty of imagination, which is synthetic and creative, while reason is only analytic. When Coleridge made the Imagination with a capital *I* "the living power and prime

---

[22] Cf. *Unpublished Letters of S. T. Coleridge*, ed. E. L. Griggs (London: Constable & Co., Ltd., 1932), I, 155-56.
[23] "Defense of Poetry." Italics added.

agent of all human perception," and described it as "a repetition in the finite mind of the eternal act of creation in the infinite I AM" he went as far as anyone could go in divinizing this power.

If, according to the Romantics, the imagination creates language and poetry, it creates truth as well. Poetry, said Blake, is the vehicle of vision, and "Vision or Imagination is a Representation of what Eternally Exists, Really and Unchangeably" outside "the things of Vegetative and Generative Nature."[24] Shelley asserted that "a poem is the very image of life expressed in its eternal truth," and for Keats "what the Imagination seizes as Beauty must be truth—whether it existed before or not." According to Carlyle, the poet penetrates "into the sacred mystery of the Universe." The German Romantic philo-

---

[24] *The Poetry and Prose of Wm. Blake*, ed. G. Keynes (London: Nonesuch Press, 1939), pp. 637-38.

sophers made the poet into a Messiah of
Nature, and Nature itself into a poem.[25]

With these revolutionary notions of
language and poetry the new concept of
myth alluded to above is born. I have already mentioned Vico and his theory of
myth as a kind of naturally poetic language. Vico was indeed the founder of a
completely new philosophy of mythology:
the view that myth is not made-up story,
which had been the older, rationalistic
view, but a necessary mode of thinking,
with a reality of its own.[26] But this hypo-
thesis of Vico's, which this philosopher of
history had applied to the past, achieved
full definition as a viable philosophy of
poetry with the systematically developed
philosophy of Romanticism. It was Schell-

---

[25] Cf. R. Wellek, *op. cit.*, I, 76 and *passim;* M.
H. Abrams, *The Mirror and the Lamp: Romantic Theory and Critical Tradition* (New
York: Oxford University Press, 1953), pp.
47 ff.
[26] Cf. E. Cassirer, *op. cit.*, II *(Mythical Thought),*
3 ff.

ing who, in his *Philosophie der Mytholo-gie,* saw myth as a symbolic expression of reality, a specific and original form of life, ultimately theological in content. The poet is conceived by this philosophy as one who has recaptured the mythic way of thinking, has returned to the primitive fusion of poetry, religion, and myth. He speaks in images, and "in images," says Hamann, "is the whole treasure of human knowledge and happiness."

These Romantic notions of language, poetry, and myth, which were developed in the late eighteenth and early nineteenth centuries in reaction to the rationalism of the Enlightenment, are re-expressed in our own continuation of this very movement, reinforced by our own reaction against the hard, dry positivism of which I spoke at the beginning of my lecture, and which in turn continues the empiricism of Bentham and Hume. Thus Allen Tate, focusing on the modern phase of literary obscurantism, speaks of that idolatrous dissolution of language from the grammar of a possible world, which results from the belief that language itself can create reality: a superstition that comes down in French from Lautréamont, Rimbaud, and Mallarmé to the Surrealists, and in English to Hart Crane, Wallace Stevens, and Dylan Thomas.[27]

We have, moreover, had in our own day, besides these continuations of nineteenth century romanticisms, the immense development of cultural anthropology and depth psychology which, together with a new interest in occult speculation, has literally revolutionized modern consciousness. Poets and critics alike demonstrate this phenomenon. The best example of the former for our English-speaking world is perhaps William Butler Yeats.

Yeats spent most of his mature life in the attempt to forge a myth to take the

[27] "The Angelic Imagination," in *The Forlorn Demon* (Chicago: Regnery, 1953), p. 61.

place of his lost religion. In poems, and particularly in a series of prose works, he set forth speculations that reached their most complicated and occult form in *A Vision* (1925). As early as 1902 he had written: "All sounds, all colours, all forms, . . . as I prefer to think, call down among us certain disembodied powers, whose footsteps over our hearts we call emotions."[28] The following year, in an essay titled "Magic," he set down his belief in three doctrines which he called "the foundations of nearly all magical practices." These were:

(1) That the borders of our minds are ever shifting, and that many minds can flow into one another, as it were, and create or reveal a single mind, a single energy. (2) That the borders of our memories are as shifting, and that our memories are a part of one great memory, the memory of Nature herself.

[28] *Ideas of Good and Evil* (London: A. H. Bullen, 1903), p. 243.

(3) That this great mind and great memory can be evoked by symbols.[29]

A Vision, finally, attempts to explicate in great detail a systematic personal mythology which Yeats, like William Blake before him, claimed to have received from spirits, and which is at the same time magical knowledge and the substance of poetic vision. In poems remarkable for their power and melodic beauty, Yeats enunciated the substance of his vision. Here are a few passages from Yeats' poems that illustrate his belief in the power of language and myth to create reality:

Words alone are certain good.

Man makes a superhuman
Mirror-resembling dream.[30]

Death and life were not
Till man made up the whole,
Made lock, stock and barrel
Out of his bitter soul,

[29] *Ibid.,* p. 29.
[30] "The Song of the Happy Shepherd."

Aye, sun and moon and star, all.[31]

Note here that language is not only valuable in an absolute sense ("Words alone are certain good"), but is literally a creative power, and that man, in virtue of his mythopoeic verbal imagination, actually *makes* the reality which he sees and feels: "Death and life were not / Till man made up the whole, . . . Aye, sun and moon and star, all." The Ego really posits the Non-Ego, in Fichte's phrase.

It is in literary criticism, however, that the fusion of language, poetry, and myth has gone farthest in our time, under the aegis of Freud and Jung and the cultural anthropologists.[32] As specimens of this ap-

---

[31] "The Tower."

[32] Cf. The summary of this phase of contemporary criticism in Wimsatt and Brooks, *op. cit.*, chap. 31, "Myth and Archetype," from which my quotations are taken. Haskell M. Block has studied the impingement of cultural anthropology on literary criticism on "Cultural Anthropology and Contemporary Literary Criticism," *Journal of Aesthetics*, XI (1952), 46-54.

proach let me mention Northrop Frye's cultivation of a kind of "literary anthropology, concerned with the way that literature is informed by preliterary categories such as ritual, myth, and folk tale"; Richard Chase's conflation of poetry and myth, already referred to; Leslie Fiedler's notion of the poet as expressing "for a whole society the ritual reasoning of its inarticulate selves"; and finally Carl Jung's assimilation of art to dream and of dream to myth. We are familiar with these views; they meet us even in the pages of popular literary reviews.

What shall we say of this massive development of the "mythological" view of linguistic and poetic operations? Curiously enough, *mythos*, the Greek form of the word from which our term derives, itself originally meant "word." And there is a now discredited theory—that of Max Mueller—that myths derived from words through a kind of allegorical etymologizing.[33] It is more likely that, as Ernst Cassirer says, myth, language, and art are at the beginning undifferentiated modes of spiritual creativity, fused with, and reciprocally influencing, one another. "Again and again," says Cassirer, "myth receives new life and wealth from language, as language does from myth. And this constant interaction and interpenetration attests the unity of the mental principle from which both sprang, and of which they are simply different expressions, different manifestations and grades."[34] Myth is

[33] Cassirer, *op. cit.*, I, 22: "Thus, because the Greek word δάφνη, signifying laurel, goes back to a Sanskrit root *ahana* signifying the dawn, the myth of Daphne, who in her flight from Apollo is transformed into a laurel tree, is essentially an image of the sun god in pursuing his bride, the dawn, who ultimately takes refuge in the bosom of her mother, the earth; because in Greek the words for men and stones (λαοί and λᾶας) resemble one another, men grow from stones in the familiar myth of Deucalion and Pyrrha."

[34] *Language and Myth*, trans. Susanne K. Langer (New York: Harper & Bros., 1946), p. 98.

primitive, illogical—it would be better to say pre-logical—and magical. It confuses *post hoc* and *juxta hoc* with *propter hoc*, the part with the whole; it analogizes things animistically; it sees everything as a rhythm of ebb and flow; it exalts number into a principle of being.[35]

It would take too long (and it is unnecessary to my theme) to illustrate all these characteristics of mythic thinking, but it might be pointed out that vestiges of it are still present in our thought and speech today. For example, the division of nouns, in many modern languages, into three genders: masculine, feminine, and neuter, must have arisen in half-mythical, half-aesthetic creation, as some manifestations of it still indicate.[36] We refer to a ship as *she* and to death (more consciously personified) as *he*. Animistic analogy, too, is still part of our language. Thus we

[35] *Philosophy of Symbolic Forms*, II, 45 ff. and *passim*.
[36] *Ibid.*, I, 298.

speak of *the foot of the mountain* and *the mouth of the river,* animistic metaphors which we no longer recognize as such. We speak of *a brilliant saying* or *a shining wit,* without being aware that such phrases originally expressed the mythical fusion of light and sound in consciousness.

If this is true of everyday speech, it is of course even more true of poetic. Poetry revels in myth, in animistic and metaphorical language. It creates words when it needs them, or makes new meanings for old words. It personifies wind and flower, sun and moon and star. It loves magic numbers. ("She had three lilies in her hand, And the stars in her hair were seven.") It revives the great mythical archetypes: Ulysses, Prometheus, Faust, Leda, Helen of Troy. To go as far as Richard Chase does, however, and assert that "myth is literature" *tout court,* is to go to Crocean extremes.[37] Myth may *be-*

[37] Cf. *Quest for Myth,* p. vi: "The central prem-

come poetry by being organized as a work
of art by a poet, but it is not, in its raw
state, poetry as such. It is a way of thinking which man engages in naturally and
inevitably before he has learnt to sort out
concepts and logical processes. Looked at
from the vantage-point of mature consciousness it is confused and obscure; yet
it is not so because it wants to be so, but
because it cannot help itself.[38] Indeed, according to Cassirer, all phases of human
activity were at some stage fused with
myth.[39]

The clarifying forces of reason and sci-

ise of this book is that myth is literature, and
therefore a matter of aesthetic experience and
the imagination."

[38] Cf. Bronislaw Malinowski, *Myth in Primitive
Psychology* (New York: Norton, 1926), p. 19:
"Studied alive, myth is not symbolic, but a
direct expression of its subject-matter; it is . . .
a narrative resurrection of primeval society,
told in satisfaction of deep religious wants,
moral cravings, social submissions, assertions,
even practical requirements."

[39] *Op. cit.*, II, xiv-xv.

ence constantly work to liberate man from myth. By rationalizing language and quantifying experience they constantly threaten the language of poetry as well. If *logos* ousts *mythos,* science and philosophy menace the existence of poetry, reducing it to that "emotive utterance" and "pseudostatement" which is all that the Logical Positivists have left of it. When Bishop Sprat, in 1667, praising the work of the Royal Society for Improving Natural Knowledge, spoke of the Society's reform of prose style as "a return back to the primitive purity and shortness, when men deliver'd so many *things* almost in an equal number of words, . . . a close, naked, natural way of speaking: positive expressions, clear senses; a native easiness: bringing all things as near the Mathematical plainness as they can,"[40] he was giving an early expression to the dichotomy between referential and emotive language which has

[40] *History of the Royal Society* (1667), p. 112.

bedeviled culture in our time. Is the only alternative to mythologism the positivism of Sprat and his present-day successors?

III.

In seeking to answer this question we must again begin with language. If we go to modern students of language like Sapir or Whatmough, we find them in agreement with the Aristotelian conception.[41] "Language," says Professor Whatmough, "is a verbal systematic symbolism. . . . A language is a conventionally transmitted and acquired system of symbols. . . . It appears likely, simply in terms of regional examination of the human brain and its functioning, that speech and 'thought' are very much connectible."[42]

---

[41] Cf. Richard McKeon, "Aristotle's Conception of Language," in *Critics and Criticism Ancient and Modern,* ed. Ronald Crane (Chicago: University of Chicago Press, 1952), pp. 176-231.

[42] Joshua Whatmough, *Language: A Modern Synthesis* (New York: Mentor Books, 1957), pp. 20, 164, 192.

"The essence of language," says Sapir similarly, "consists in the assigning of conventional, voluntarily articulated sounds, or of their equivalents, to the diverse elements of experience. . . . Language and our thought-grooves are, in a sense, one and the same."[43] That is to say, words are conventional signs of mental phenomena: sensations, feelings, images, volitions, ideas and judgments, themselves responses to experience. The uses of language are naturally manifold. Whatmough divides them into four chief. Any utterance, he says, may be (1) *informative*, referential, concerned with setting forth the facts of a situation; (2) *dynamic*, intended to form opinion; (3) *emotive*, directed to move others to action; (4) *aesthetic*, discourse "manifested chiefly but not solely in poetry and other deliberately cultivated styles."[44] Note here his distinction between

[43] Edward Sapir, *Language* (New York: Harcourt Brace, 1949), pp. 11, 217.
[44] *Ibid.*, 86-88.

the emotive use of language, which is to
the Logical Positivist the only alternative
to the referential and scientific, and the
aesthetic, where "we have perception and
appraisal of an abstract and subjective
kind."[45] This is the point that concerns us
here, for if language is a system of signs
standing for meanings, then even aesthetic
discourse, even poetry, as a linguistic art,
must use words as signs of meaning, "deliberately."

But if language is a system of conventional symbols, it still remains true, and
must be emphasized, that these symbols
are not all of the same sort. Some—ejacu-
lations like "Oh," "Ah," "Alas," and the
famous "Nuts" of General McAuliffe—are
close to the "natural sign," as logicians call
it—like the smoke which is the sign of fire.
Others, because of their imaginative and
emotional connotations, achieve meaning
through sound, context, and association—
as in Keats' famous

[45] *Ibid.*, 88.

> magic casements opening on the foam
> Of perilous seas in faery-lands forlorn

—where the meaning is resonant of much more than the individual words lexically signify. Others again, like the abstract technical terms of the scientist and the logician, approach as closely to pure abstraction as language is able to come, and even transform themselves finally into the rarefied symbolism of algebra. Poetry uses all these levels of speech, but particularly the first two.

In an essay he wrote many years ago, "Sign and Symbol," Jacques Maritain made a distinction "of capital importance," as he said, between the *logical* sign and the *magical* sign:

> I describe sign as a 'logical sign' . . . when it is located in a certain functional status, wherein it is a sign for the *intelligence* (speculative or practical) taken as the *dominant factor* of the psychic regime or of the regime of culture. . . . I describe sign as a 'magical sign,' or as

a sign of the sphere of the Dream, when it is located in another functional status, wherein it is a sign *for the imagination* taken as a supreme or *dominant factor* of all psychic life or of all the life of culture.[46]

This is a valuable distinction if it is not pushed too far. It is true that we live now in the state of Logos, as Maritain calls it, that is to say, a state in which intelligence is the dominant factor of human life, individual and social, and that the naive state of man, when man and Nature were one, as Schiller put it, is a condition we neither can nor ought to revert to, if indeed there ever was such a state.[47] But Maritain himself hastens to add that "in the daylight

---

[46] "Sign and Symbol," in *Ransoming the Time*, translated by Harry L. Binsse (New York: Scribner, 1941), pp. 227-28. (This essay originally appeared in French in 1938.) Cf. also Maritain's more recent *Philosophy of History* (New York: Scribner, 1957), pp. 96-104.

[47] Cf. Frank Kermode, *Romantic Image* (New York: Routledge and Paul, 1957), 138 ff. for a critique of what T. S. Eliot called "dis-

regime of the primacy of Logos, whatever
was *vital* in magical thought remains,"
even if "what was magical as such disap-
pears."[48]

What is it that was "vital in magical
thought" if not the activity of the imagination generating a play of images to con-
cretize dimly apprehended modes of being? Is not this what happens when
man really experiences thought, especially
when such thought is about the elemental,
the recondite, and the incomprehensible?
Plato himself, though he contemned poetry, had to resort to myth when he tried
to speak about the nature of the soul and
the afterlife. The poet is only a man, and
when he tries to express thoughts and
feelings so as to give them their full human reality he must use language in all its
power and suggestiveness, and this means

sociation of sensibility"—the modern equivalent of Schiller's primitivistic aesthetic.
[48] *Op. cit.*, 250.

to speak in a way which transcends the logical sign. More of this later.

One must distinguish clearly, to be sure, between such inevitably human ways of expression and the attempt to return to some preconscious state, whether that of the individual or that of the race, a pathological process characteristic of some modern poets. Such myths as those of racism or sexual innocence, for example, which contaminate science itself, and which abound in our literature, especially today in the novel (cf. D. H. Lawrence), are in reality very different from a return to primitive mentality as that is described by anthropologists. Such attempted regressions represent a morbid kind of behavior, "and it would be doing primitive man an injury," as Maritain says, "were one to seek therein an equivalent to their mythology." When the poet thinks mythically, he must do so as an artist, using the resources of the imagination and of language deliberately, not denaturing them to recapture a hypothetical prelogical state.

The state of Logos has further claims on the poet. If he cannot regress to a pre-logical state save at the risk of his sanity— we remember Arthur Rimbaud's " I say that one must be a seer, must make him-self a seer. The poet makes himself a seer through a long, immense, and de-liberate derangement of all the senses"[49] —it is even worse for him to mistake his primitivistic imaginings for vision into the depths of reality, to believe that he can create myths that will function as sur-rogates for philosophy and religion. In an important footnote in his fascinating re-cent volume, *Creative Intuition in Art and Poetry*, Maritain (who has become more and more interested in the subject) has diagnosed and dissolved the pretensions

[49] "Lettre du Voyant" ("Je dis qu'il faut être voyant, se faire voyant. Le Poëte se fait voyant par un long, immense et raisonné *dérèglement de tous les sens*.")

to magical clairvoyant powers which certain modern poets have assumed, and which critics in turn have accorded them. Pointing out that the need to create new myths arises from a more fundamental fact than the obsolescence of poetic traditions, namely, from the void of beliefs in which the modern poet finds himself, he shows that the poet's "laboring and straining to find new myths for the sake of art, or considering the invention of new myths a direct requirement and a proper task of poetry itself," involves a double and serious illusion. For, in the first place, the *metaphysical* myths under discussion are the organic signs of some real faith; they are symbols "through which a conviction of the entire soul nourishes and quickens from within the very power of creative imagination. Such myths have no force except through the faith man has in them." The effort of a poet to create new metaphysical beliefs for the sake of his work as a poet "is self-contradictory, since, having invented them, he cannot believe in them. . . . Metaphysical myths are needed by poetry, but they cannot be provided by poetry." In the second place, poetry needs the metaphysical myths present in the poet's mind only indirectly and extrinsically: "These beliefs and metaphysical myths matter *directly* to him, not for his poetry but for his own human self, his metaphysical situation in the mystery of being, and his way of working out his own destiny."[50]

This is a body blow to poets and theorists who want the poet to assume the role of religious teacher or *shaman,* to whom—in the words of Matthew Arnold, who first stated this notion plainly in English—we shall have to turn for an interpretation of life, "the religious language of the human race" being "in truth poetry, which it mis-

[50] (New York: Pantheon Books, 1953), pp. 180-81, note 33.

takes for science."[51] It is a notion that is still prevalent in certain quarters today.

Is the poet, then, to be reduced to versifying platitudes or inventing insubstantial fictions? There could be a worse fate for him. He might become the writer of *Chants de Maldoror*.[52] Better to versify platitudes, one might well say, than to perpetrate nonsense, to amuse children than to bore adults. But I do not think that we have to force him to choose between these two alternatives.

The old name (and the etymological meaning) of "poet" was "maker." According to this tradition the poet is a maker of poems, a practitioner of the art of poetry;

[51] "The Study of Poetry." Cf. also *Literature and Dogma* (New York: Macmillan, 1924). Cf. Vincent Buckley's recent study, *Poetry and Morality: Studies in the Criticism of Matthew Arnold, T. S. Eliot, and F. R. Leavis* (London, Chatto and Windus, 1959), Chap. II.

[52] A long, obscure, hallucinatory "prose poem" by the writer who called himself "le Comte de Lautréamont." His real name was Isidore Ducasse (1846-1870).

he is not primarily a provider of knowledge or a discoverer of truth. Knowing—
doing—making—of these three activities he
engages, *qua* poet, in making. He is, as
such, more concerned with making de-
signs in language than with communicat-
ing knowledge. Robert Frost speaks of
"the figure a poem makes,"[53] and Gerard
Manley Hopkins says: "Poetry is speech
framed for contemplation of the mind . . .
for its own sake and interest over and
above meaning. Some matter and meaning is essential, but only as an element
necessary to support the shape which is
contemplated for its own sake."[54] This primacy of the element of art in poetry is
something that both poets and critics have
occasionally forgotten. (It must be added,
in parenthesis, that they have occasionally

---

[53] Introduction to *Collected Poems* (New York:
Holt & Co., 1939).
[54] *The Notebooks and Papers of Gerard Manley
Hopkins,* ed. H. House (Oxford University
Press, 1937), p. 249.

remembered it too well, as when Archibald Macleish wrote: "A poem should not *mean* / But *be*," which is nonsense when you consider that a poem's being, apart from the sounds it makes, *is* precisely its meaning; for, considered as a physical object, a poem is a pretty unfleshed skeleton!—a statue has three dimensions, a painting two, but a poem has only one: time.)

There is, however, beside the tradition of the poet as maker, another and older tradition, which sees in the poet a *vates* —a seer or prophet.[55] The Greeks distinguished the ἀοιδός from the ποιητής.[56] The ancient Celts, Robert Graves tells us,

---

[55] L. *vates*, probably related to FA, root of *for*, *fari* (speak, say), and Gr. φα, whence φάσχω, φημί. The Latin word may be of Celtic origin —cf. Ir. *fáith* (poet), Welsh *gwawd* (song of praise). Cf. Skr. *api-vátati* (he understands).

[56] Gr. ἀοιδός (singer, minstrel, bard); ἀοιδή, Attic ᾠδή, (song). ἀείδω, Ionic and poetic form used by Homer, Pindar, etc. [ἀϜείδω (sing, chant). Cf. Skr. *vadati* (speaks)].

carefully distinguished the poet, who
was originally a priest and judge as well,
and whose person was sacrosanct, from
the mere gleeman. He was in Irish called
fili, seer, in Welsh *derwydd*, or oak-
seeker, which is the probable derivation
of "Druid." . . . In ancient Ireland the
ollave, or master-poet, sat next to the
king. . . . His chief interest was the refinement of complex poetic truth to exact statement.[57]

The Christian Revelation took from the
pagan bard his office as seer in the religious sense, but with the decline of faith
in the Enlightenment the Romantics, as
we saw, sought to revive the notion of
the vatic poet (recall Blake and Shelley),
and the later nineteenth century went so
far as to make all the arts epiphanies of
the artist's very self-consciousness: self-

---

[57] *The White Goddess: A Historical Grammar
of Poetic Myth* (New York: Vintage Books,
1958), pp. 8-10. There is a great deal of curi-
ous erudition and occult speculation in this
book.

consciousness itself became prophetic and creative. And here again Maritain has been before me, much of his *Creative Intuition* being devoted to demonstrating just this phenomenon.[58]

Is the poet a "maker"? Is the poet a "seer"? Or is he both? In a certain sense, which I shall develop, it seems to me that an affirmative answer to the third question is the correct one.

As a matter of fact, the tradition of the poet-*vates* was never, until very recently, disconnected from a strong emphasis on the poet as maker. Empedocles composed his rhapsody *On Nature* in careful hexa-

---

[58] Paul Valéry, in turn, was before Maritain in realizing the autistic character of modern poetry. Cf. his *Art of Poetry,* trans. Denise Folliot (New York: Pantheon Books, 1958), p. 40: "Finally, towards the middle of the nineteenth century, we see asserting itself in our literature a remarkable will to isolate Poetry once for all from every other essence than itself." Valéry ascribes the initiative in this movement to Edgar Allan Poe, long recognized as the father of "Symbolisme."

meters. The Irish ollave, as we saw, had
as his chief interest "the refinement of
complex poetic truth to exact statement."
The elevated place assigned the poet in
Renaissance culture was due not only to
his powers of vision but equally to his
education and his mastery of his craft.
Milton, in that great passage in which he
predicts his own epic, speaks of "a work
not to be raised from the heat of youth,
or the vapours of wine, . . . nor to be ob-
tained by the invocation of Dame Memory and her Siren daughters, but by devout
prayer to that eternal Spirit who can enrich with all utterance and knowledge,"
but continues without interruption: "to
this must be added industrious and select
reading, steady observation, insight into
all seemly and generous arts and affairs."[59]
And Dryden, though he held the poet to
be a sacred minister, and an epic poem

[59] "The Reason of Church Government," in *John
Milton: Prose Selections,* ed. M. Y. Hughes
(New York: Doubleday, 1947), pp. 109-110.

"undoubtedly the greatest work which the soul of man is capable to perform,"[60] concerned himself, as we know, equally with the techniques and the theory of his art."[61]

It was only after the German Idealists had literally arrogated creation to human consciousness, that maker and seer flew apart, and the poet began to crave magical knowledge. I have already cited Rimbaud's famous pronouncement—"I say that one must be a seer. The poet makes himself a seer through a long, immense, and deliberate derangement of all the senses" —a *deliberate* invitation to chaos. But what happens, we ask with Maritain, "if poetry yields to an invasion of vertigo"? "Then it

---

[60] "Dedication of the Aeneis."
[61] Cf. his reply to Settle: "A man should be learned in several sciences, and should have a reasonable, philosophical, and in some measure a mathematical head, to be a complete and excellent poet." L. I. Bredvold, *The Best of Dryden* (New York: Nelson, 1933), p. xii. Cf. also Dryden's prefatory essays to his poems.

is cut off from any operative end. Breaking its natural ties, and driven back on itself in an unnatural movement of inversion, it only yearns to *know*."[62] Poetry thus parts company with art as a practical virtue of the intellect; it yearns to *know*, not to *make*. It loses interest in beauty. It seeks power, magical knowledge. The end, then, can only be a parody of revelation brought about by the disorganization of man's mental and moral organism, releasing the forces of the unconscious. "The delectation that beauty gives is replaced by the delight of the experience of supreme freedom in the night of subjectivity."[63]

If we accept this Rimbaldian idea of art and poetry, we are lost in pure relativism and subjectivism. "Creative intuition" as such is not subject to review or critical judgment. Maritain, despite his revulsion

---

[62] *Creative Intuition in Art and Poetry,* p. 186.
[63] *Ibid.,* 189.

from the irrationality of much modern art, makes out a strong case for it, allocating the essence of the process to the "poetic sense" and allowing for a high degree of obscurity so long as the "poetic sense" is present. In some modern poems, he says, "our intelligence is aware of the existence of a signification, but the signified remains unknown. . . . The fact that what is signified is unknown is almost the fact that the sign signifies the unknown."[64] On these terms, it seems to me, nothing further can be said about the relation of poetry to truth.[65]

[64] *Ibid.*, 266.

[65] Has Jacques Maritain been influenced by his wife Raïssa in some of his thinking on art and —especially—poetry? The little volume, *Situation de la Poésie*, which they published in 1938 [(Paris: Desclée De Brouwer) translated by Marshall Suther as *The Situation of Poetry*, (New York: Philosophical Library, 1955)], contains two essays by Raïssa Maritian, "Sense and Non-Sense in Poetry," and "Magic, Poetry, and Mysticism," in which the notion of "poetic sense" is first developed.

On the other hand, it ought to be stressed
that, in any philosophical account of the
matter, there is acknowledgement of an
element of mystery, of "creative intuition"
or "inspiration" or some similar alogical
activity in the production of poetry (when
it is thought of as more than mere versifi-
cation). Even Aristotle and St. Thomas
admit this—and before them of course
Plato, who, however, approved of no one's
poetry but his own. Aristotle, "who some-
times," according to Butcher, "writes as if
the faculty of the logician were enough to
construct a poem, says 'poetry is a thing
inspired.' "[66] In the *Poetics* the Stagirite
distinguishes the εὔπλαστος—the poet of
flexible genius, and the ἐκστατικός—the
ecstatic poet with eyes "in fine frenzy roll-
ing."[67] And St. Thomas, who had no very
high notion of poetry, having been trained

---

[66] S. H. Butcher, *Aristotle's Theory of Poetry and
Fine Art* (London: Macmillan, 1932), pp.
396-97.

[67] *Poetics*, xvii, 2: "διὸ εὐφυοῦς ἡ ποιητική ἐστιν ἢ

in the dialectically dominated trivium of
his day (though, let me hasten to add, he
was no mean poet himself),[68] compares
poetic knowledge to theological, both
using the symbolic mode of discourse,
cum neutra rationi proportionetur—since

μανικοῦ. τούτων γὰρ οἱ μὲν εὔπλαστοι οἱ δὲ ἐκστατικοί
εἰσιν." ("Hence poetry implies either a happy
gift of nature or a strain of madness. In the
one case a man can take the mould of any
character; in the other, he is lifted out of his
proper self."—Butcher's translation) It must
be stated that recent commentators disagree
on the meaning of this passage. Cf. Gerald F.
Else, *Aristotle's Poetics: The Argument* (Cambridge: Harvard University Press, 1957), pp.
486 ff.

[68] Cf. C. S. Baldwin, *Medieval Rhetoric and
Poetic* (New York: Macmillan, 1928), p. 151:
"At the fall of Rome the Trivium was dominated by *rhetorica,* in the Carolingian period
by *grammatica,* in the high middle age by
dialectica. The shift to logic probably began
in the eleventh century." (For an evaluation
of St. Thomas Aquinas as a poet, cf. F. J. E.
Raby, *A History of Christian Latin Poetry
from the Beginnings to the Close of the Middle Ages* [2nd ed.; Oxford: Clarendon Press,
1953], 405 ff.)

neither is proportionate to reason.[69] Father
Duffy, indeed, in his *Philosophy of Poetry
Based on Thomistic Principles*, applies the
six kinds of contemplation according to
which the mind may ascend through crea-
tures to the Creator (which St. Thomas
himself had taken from Richard of St.
Victor) to poetry, seeing the poet as en-
gaged in one or several of these types of
vision.[70]

[69] *Scriptum Super Libros Sententiarum Magistri
Petri Lombardi*, ed. R. P. Mandonnet (Paris:
P. Lethielleux, 1929), p. 18: "Poetica scientia
est de his quae propter defectum veritatis non
possunt a ratione capi; unde oportet quod
quasi similitudinibus ratio seducatur: theologia autem est de his quae supra rationem
sunt; et ideo modus symbolicus utrique com-
munis est, cum neutra rationi proportionetur."
[70] Rev. John Duffy, CSSR (Washington, D.C.:
Catholic University Press, 1945), pp. 149-151.
The Thomistic text in question is *Summa
Theologiae*, II-II, q. 180, a. 4, obj. 3: "Rich-
ardus de Sancto Victore . . . distinguit sex
species contemplationum: quarum prima est
secundum solam imaginationem, dum attendi-
mus res corporales; secunda autem est in imaginatione, secundum rationem, prout scilicet

If, then, poetry is not primarily an affair of reason—and we must conclude, as everyone before us *has* concluded, and as our own reflection will attest, that it is not —it still remains a fact that it is uniquely a work of man, and man is by definition a rational creature, or at least, in Lactantius' phrase, *capax rationis*. Language, moreover, which is the special prerogative of this rational creature (no mere animal is capable of it), is likewise the medium

sensibilium ordinem et dispositionem consideramus; tertia est in imaginatione secundum rationem, quando scilicet per inspectionem rerum visibilium ad invisibilia sublevamur; quarta autem est in ratione secundum rationem, quando scilicet animus intendit invisibilibus, quae imaginatione non novit; quinta autem est supra rationem, non tamen praeter rationem, quando ex divina revelatione cognoscimus ea quae humana ratione comprehendi non possunt. Sexta autem est supra rationem, et praeter rationem, quando scilicet ex divina illuminatione cognoscimus ea quae rationi repugnare videntur, sicut ea quae dicuntur de mysterio Trinitatis."

of poetry. Poetry is therefore instinct with
the intelligence of its efficient cause.

What, then, is its relation to truth? The
question of the truth of poetry is an old
one. Plato raised it early, and answered
it negatively. He denied poetry any claim
to truth, in both the logical and the moral
senses of the word:—the logical, because
poetry, according to him, imitates an imi-
tation of reality and is thus thrice removed
from the truth of the Ideas;—the moral,
because poetry is a lie, a fiction that "feeds
and waters the passions instead of drying
them up."[71]

Aristotle was the better philosopher
here. He saw that poetry grew out of
man's mimetic and harmonic instincts, and
that, though dealing in fictions, it was akin
to philosophy in its adumbration of the
universal; "Poetry therefore is more philosophical than history, for poetry tends to
express the universal, while history de-

[71] *Republic*, X, 595-607.

scribes the particular."[72] This is still the
briefest and most straightforward statement of poetry's claim to truth. But it
must be interpreted, it seems to me, in
Goethe's fashion.

[72] Poetics, ix, 3: "διὸ καὶ φιλοσοφώτερον καὶ
σπουδαιότερον ποίησις ἱστορίας ἐστίν: ἡ μὲν γὰρ
ποίησις μᾶλλον τὰ καθόλου, ἡ δ' ἱστορία τὰ καθ'
ἕκαστον λέγει." Cf. Butcher, op. cit., Chap.
III ("Poetic Truth"). Else (op. cit., 302
ff.) seems to me wrong-headed in his com-
mentary on this passage. "These notions of
the 'philosophical' content of poetry," he says
(p. 302), "grow out of the concept that the
work of art must be *beautiful*. Poetic truth
is a corollary of poetic beauty. The structure
of events 'built' by the poet, in order to be
beautiful, must be a unified and complete
whole." This is true enough, but not relevant
here; Aristotle is not talking about beauty in
this passage—he discusses it in 1450b-1451a.
What he says here is that poetry is more
philosophical than history because it aims at
the universal. Later on in his discussion (p.
305) Else does get around to admitting that
poetry "can offer us . . . a view of the *typology
of human nature*, freed from the accidents that
encumber our vision in real life." This is to
return to Butcher's interpretation, which Else
had earlier (p. 302) rejected. For Aristotle's

It makes a great difference whether the
poet seeks the particular for the universal or beholds the universal in the
particular. From the first procedure
originates allegory, when the particular
is considered only as an illustrating, as
an example of the universal. The latter,
however, is properly the nature of poetry: it expresses something particular
without thinking of the universal or
pointing to it. Whoever grasps this particular in a living way will simultane-
ously perceive the universal too, without
even becoming aware of it—or realize
it only later.[73]

notion of the universal (τὸ κάθολον) cf. W. D.
Ross, *Aristotle* (5th ed.; London: Methuen,
1949), pp. 157 ff.; Alfred Gudeman's com-
mentary on the *Poetics* (Berlin: W. de Gruyter
& Co., 1934), pp. 206-7; Jan Lukasiewicz,
Aristotle's Syllogistic (2nd ed.; Oxford: Clarendon Press, 1957), p. 1.

[73] J. W. Goethe, *Maxims and Reflections*, No.
279. Cf. Karl Vietor, *Goethe* (Bern: A. Franke
Ag. Verlag, 1949), p. 162. The problem of
poetry and truth has exercised modern critical
theory continually. Recent treatments of it
may be found in the following: Louis A. Reid,
A Study of Aesthetics (London: G. Allen &

Such an interpretation avoids the confusion of poetry with philosophy, for, if poetry is philosophi*cal*, it is not philoso*phy*.
There *are*, to be sure, such things as

Unwin, 1931), pp. 249 ff. ("Art, Truth and
Reality"); Louis Harap, "What Is Poetic
Truth?" *The Journal of Philosophy*, XXX
(1933), 441-48; D. G. James, *Scepticism and
Poetry* (London: G. Allen and Unwin, 1937);
Dorothy Walsh, "The Cognitive Content of
Art," *Philosophical Review*, LII (1943), 433-
451; John Hospers, *Meaning and Truth in the
Arts* (Chapel Hill, N.C.: University of North
Carolina Press, 1946); Wm. J. Rooney, *The
Problem of 'Poetry and Belief' in Contempo-
rary* Criticism (Washington, D.C.: Catholic
University of America Press, 1949); Morris
Weitz, "Art, Language, and Truth," in *The
Problems of Aesthetics*, ed. E. Vivas and M.
Krieger (New York: Rinehart, 1953); Alfred
Adler, "In What Sense Can Poetic Meaning
Be Verified," *Essays in Criticism*, II (Oxford,
1952); Martin Jarret-Kerr, *Studies in Litera-
ture and Belief* (London: Rockliff, 1954);
Eliseo Vivas, "Literature and Knowledge," in
Creation and Discovery (New York: Noon-
day Press, 1955); C. Day Lewis, *The Poet's
Way of Knowledge* (Cambridge: 1957); M.
H. Abrams (ed.), *Literature and Belief*, (New
York: Columbia University Press, 1958).

philosophical poems in the technical sense of that adjective, *e.g.*, the *De Rerum Natura,* Pope's *Essay on Man,* Robert Bridges' *Testament of Beauty;* but these are a species by themselves. If poetry *qua* poetry is philosophical, it is because it is a significant as well as an aesthetic representation. What does it signify? Some aspect of reality as the poet sees and feels it. "It is the attempt," says Paul Valéry, "to represent, or to restore, by means of articulated language, those things, or that thing, which cries, tears, caresses, kisses, sighs, etc., try obscurely to express, and which objects seem to want to express in all that is lifelike in them or appears to have design.[74] If this vision, this poetic experience, is to be objectified as a work of art and made communicable, it must,

---

[74] Paul Valéry, *Selected Writings,* trans. Louise Varèse (New York: New Directions, 1950), p. 147. Valéry is, his tendency to solipsism apart, one of the most subtle and perspicacious of modern poetic theorists.

in its expression, transcend pure subjectivity. The *magical* sign, to use Maritain's term, must yield to, or at least implicate, the *logical*. It cannot be "a sign for the imagination taken as a supreme or dominant factor of all psychic life or of all the life of culture." We are living in the state of Logos, not of Magic. Even the poet is. He cannot pretend to be a kind of contemporary ancestor without risking his sanity, or at least without being at odds with himself. For it is certainly undesirable to lose one's reason deliberately. Herbert Read says of the artist Turner that "he lacked the final courage, the courage to take leave of his senses."[75] That is a kind of courage most of us, I think, would pray to be spared.

The uneasy attitude of the philosopher toward the poet is nevertheless justified.

[75] "Surrealism and the Romantic Principle," in Mark Schorer, Josephine Miles, Gordon McKenzie, *Criticism* (New York: Harcourt, Brace, 1948), p. 106.

"There is an ancient quarrel between philosophy and poetry," remarked the Socrates of Plato's *Republic*, in what seems to us the morning glory of our culture. In matters of philosophy, as Walter Kaufmann points out in his excellent recent treatment of the subject, poets are suspect, "and it is foolish to suppose that a great poet must be, probably is, a great philosopher or thinker. On the contrary, it is inherently unlikely. . . . The beauty of a line or passage is no warrant of the truth of its assertion."[76]

Philosophy, indeed, begins as critical reflection on the thoughts of poets, as Greek speculation testifies, and as nineteenth century German thought shows most plainly.[77] "One of its central tasks," says Kaufmann of philosophy, "is always to show up

---

[76] *From Shakespeare to Existentialism* (Boston: Beacon Press, 1959), p. 248.

[77] Cf. *Ibid.*, p. 55: "Nineteenth century German philosophy consisted to a considerable extent in a series of efforts to assimilate the phenomenon of Goethe."

the illicit pretensions of poets and the
would-be poets who mistake their fan-
tasies for truth. . . . The philosopher is the
gadfly who will not allow men to drowse
languidly in the dusk of murky sentiment
and comfortable prejudice: he wakes them
up and casts a glaring shaft of light into
the twilight of imagination."[78]

But philosophy cannot clarify everything, even so.

> Whenever it makes clear a few things,
> much else remains in semidarkness—
> and it is the poet who reminds us of this,
> drawing freely on the riches of the vast
> periphery of shadows. . . . Poets are not
> philosophical oracles. Yet

—and I am still quoting from Kaufmann,
and here very much to the point—

> they have not only the gift of lending ex-
> pression to single feelings and attitudes,
> but also the power to create characters,
> enabling the reader to gain experiences

[78] *Ibid.*, p. 253.

for which any possibility would otherwise be lacking in a single human life. Poetry makes possible a vast expansion of our world, an extension of sympathy, and a profounder understanding not only of human possibilities but of human realities. Poetry can supplement philosophy best when it quite renounces the attempt to offer mystic truths and instead confronts us with what reason can never fully comprehend [we are reminded of St. Thomas' comparison of *poetica scientia* and *theologia*]: above all, with man's inexhaustible potentialities, and with that aspect of experience which language can never fully grasp so long as it does not make use of all its resources.[79]

The danger is that when the poet uses language he also lets language use him, for, as the same writer says, "poetry is an expression of the love of language, and when the beloved is used as a mere means, love has ceased."[80] What the poet writes

[79] *Ibid.*, p. 254.
[80] *Ibid.*, p. 246.

is not always what he planned. As an artist in language he is stimulated as well as limited by the nature of his medium. He follows the suggestions of image and sound, rhyme and rhythm, allusion and association. He is particularly addicted to metaphor, as Aristotle already observed when he said of the poet: "But the greatest thing by far is to have a command of metaphor. This alone cannot be imparted by another; it is the mark of genius, for to make good metaphors implies an eye for resemblance."[81] Metaphor is at the very heart of language, for every language is, as has often been remarked, an unconscious tissue of petrified metaphors. The poet thinks metaphors anew, thus revivifying imagination and speech and restoring them to their pristine power. Indeed, what *was* originally myth becomes metaphor; what *was* truth (*Fuit haec sapientia quondam*—this was wisdom once upon a time—

[81] *Poetics*, XXII, 9.

said Horace of the mythic lore of legendary Greece) becomes poetry.

Modern criticism has realized this again, after centuries of literary Cartesianism had drained the lifeblood from language and substituted galvanization for animation. Listen to a once famous eighteenth century rhetorician and literary critic speak of "simple" and "literary" language. This is what he says: "Simple expression just makes our ideas known to others; but figurative language, over and above, bestows a particular dress upon that idea: a dress, which both makes it to be remarked, and adorns it."[82] The idea in its naked clarity and distinctness is dressed up by figurative language to become poetry! This dichotomy of "idea" and "literary" expression may still persist in some of our text-

---

[82] Hugh Blair, *Lectures on Rhetoric and Belles Lettres* (1783). Cited by Walter J. Ong, S.J., "The Meaning of the New Criticism," in *Twentieth Century English,* ed. Wm. S. Knickerbocker (New York: The Philosophical Library, 1946), p. 346.

books today, but the living school of contemporary criticism has long outgrown it. We no longer look on words as mere counters, hard and definite as metal coins, to be handed about from mind to mind, but rather as parts of contexts which influence when they do not define their meanings. That is how poetry is possible. The unity of a poem, as Walter Ong says, is not explicable in terms of the organization of ideas in their own light. Such a unity would, to be strictly logical, require the necessary connections of the logic of demonstration. The logic of rhetoric is less unified. And

the logic of poetry is still more sliding, for the concepts here are merely juxtaposed, united, as St. Thomas says, by our supposing (*existimatio*). We have not in poetry even the justification of the historian for uniting concepts. The historian lacks logical necessity but has contingent actuality on his side. . . . In poetry we have a very weak analogue of logic and no contingent actuality at all. . . . The poem holds abstractions in its unity through their connections with the material elements which enter into it. Ultimately, . . . the logic of poetry is unified in a particular act of contemplation, an act peculiar to man and involving, in unusually close cooperation, the interplay of the sensory and the intellectual that is necessary for the kind of knowledge which must be had by a being dealing with the intelligible existing in matter.[83]

And here I ought, if there were time, to enlarge on the logic of poetry—the way in which poetry uses language. However, only extended enumeration and analysis of concrete examples could begin to do justice to this phase of the subject. It has, indeed, been treated at length by others, and I must leave it at that.[84]

[83] *Ibid.*, 355-56.
[84] I. A. Richards [*Practical Criticism*, (London: Kegan Paul, 1921)] was one of the first critics to demonstrate the complexity and subtlety of poetic language. Wm. Empson, especially in his *Seven Types of Ambiguity* (London:

But let us not forget that there is another kind of truth besides logical truth, whether in the strict sense or in that of poetic logic, and it is this other kind that concerns the poet as artist particularly. For, like the painter, the composer, the

Chatto and Windus, 1930), examined the oblique language of poetry with a penetration at times over-ingenious. G. R. Hamilton [*Poetry and Contemplation: A New Preface to Poetics* (Cambridge: Cambridge University Press, 1938)] has valuable insights. Perhaps the best study of the specific problem of the language of poetry is Owen Barfield's *Poetic Diction: A Study in Meaning* (2nd edition; London: Faber and Faber, 1951). Many of the American "New Critics" have specialized in contextualist analyses of poems. Among them the following may be singled out: R. P. Blackmur *(The Expense of Greatness*, 1940); Cleanth Brooks *(The Well Wrought Urn*, 1947); Allen Tate *(The Forlorn Demon*, 1952); Wm. K. Wimsatt *(The Verbal Icon*, 1954). A brilliant recent study is Earl K. Wasserman's *The Subtler Language* (Baltimore: The Johns Hopkins Press, 1959). David I. Masson has been doing excellent work in studying the sound-sense relationship in poetry; cf. his "Vowel and Consonant Patterns in Poetry," *Journal of Aesthetics*, XII (December, 1953), 213-227.

sculptor, the poet is interested first of all, precisely because he is an artist, in the work to be made. And this work is a work of art rather than science, is *techné* rather than *logos*. The truth the poet is primarily concerned with, then, is the truth of his work, its conformity to his artistic intention—the *recta ratio factibilium* or "working idea."[85] This is ontological truth, the truth of the existent that is the work of art, in this case the poem. Etienne Gilson, in the book that marks his entrance into the field of philosophy of art, says:

> In speaking of artistic truth, a poet means to say that something that was but an indistinct and shadowy image in his mind has become a concrete reality in his work. A completed poem is a dream come true. In Keats' own words: 'The Imagination may be compared to Adam's dream—he awoke and found it truth.' Eve is the truth of Adam's dream:

[85] It seems unnecessary at this late date to rehearse the scholastic metaphysics of art as developed by Maritain and others.

> Eve, that is, not the image of reality, but the reality of an image.[86]

It could not be expressed better.

This truth of existence, or ontological truth, of the work of art need not mean correspondence to actually existing reality, though, since whatever is in the mind was first in the senses, which are our avenues of contact with the reality about us, it is impossible to conceive of an artifact that is entirely novel, entirely without resemblance to actual existents. It is certainly impossible to conceive of such a contingency in the case of poetry, the medium of this art, language, being essentially a system of signs—and how can there be signs without the signified, that is, signs without meanings that are specified and defined by existents? The words in a poem, one must say, are at the same time signs *and* objects—carriers of images organized

---

[86] *Painting and Reality* (New York: Pantheon Books, 1957), p. 154.

"in a living and independent body; they cannot give place to synonyms without causing the sense of the poem to suffer or die."[87] But they still remain signs. "It is not in order to communicate ideas, it is to maintain contact with the universe of intuitiveness that they must remain signs."[88] If they lose this contact, they are non-*sense*, that is to say, *nonsense*.

It is difficult but, I think, not impossible to keep these distinctions clear. It is in any case of prime importance to do so, for, unless we keep them clear we shall wander forever in the fog and confusion of half-truths. If we deny to poetry all access to truth in the logical sense, we obviously contradict the testimony of human history as well as that of our own experience. And yet, if we demand of it the kind and degree of logical truth that science and philosophy aim at, we rarely if ever get it. For

[87] Raïssa Maritain, "Sense and Non-Sense in Poetry," p. 2. See n. 65 above.
[88] *Ibid.*, p. 3.

the meanings which poetry makes are pos-
ited not in the mode of logic but in that
of language—language conceived as a
complex, vital function of the human organism, which involves imagination and
the feelings as well as reason. And some-
times there is not much of the latter. A
poem may be about little more than the
fascination of Julia's clothes, or the meaning of a bracelet of hair about the wrist,
or the comedy of a social *contretemps*
like the snipping off of a young lady's lock
of hair, and still survive as a masterpiece
while ambitious tomes on the laws of matter or the constitution of the cosmos are
discarded after a few years.[89] Or it may,

[89] Cf. Thomas De Quincey, "The Literature of
Knowledge and the Literature of Power," in
Schorer *et al., Criticism,* p. 475: "The very
highest work that has ever existed in the literature of knowledge is but a *provisional* work:
a book upon trial and sufferance, and *quamdiu
bene se gesserit.* Let its teaching be even par-
tially revised, let it be but expanded, nay, even
let its teaching be but placed in a better order, and instantly it is superseded. Whereas

indeed, be about heaven and hell and the sum of man's life on earth, like Dante's and Milton's epics or the two parts of Goethe's *Faust*. All kinds of poems have in common this one thing, if little else, that they are works of art in language, possessing the ontological truth of their existence as works of art.[90]

the feeblest works in the literature of power, surviving at all, survive as finished and unalterable amongst men."

[90] In 1931 the Polish philosopher Roman Ingarden published *Das Literarische Kunstwerk* (Halle: M. Niemeyer, 1931), the most thorough analysis of the mode of existence of the literary work of art to date. Ingarden approaches the literary work phenomenologically. He finds it to exist in a stratified form, a polyphony of values, beginning with the phonetic surface, then the meaning units underlying the word sounds, the represented objects underlying these, the views and attitudes implied, and finally the author's "world" —the metaphysical qualities at the center of the work. The literary work of art is thus, in René Wellek's summary of this theory, "a system of norms of ideal concepts which are intersubjective, . . . accessible only through individual mental experiences, based on the

If, then, the Positivist dismisses poetry, as he does ethics and metaphysics, as "pseudo-statement" and "emotive utterance," and the Mythologist raises it to mystical and obscure heights—or depths, the sober humanist in the tradition of Aristotle and the Realists sees it, not indeed as logic or as esoteric revelation, but as a human activity of ancient origin and perduring value. And he sees the poet as a unique but very human being: a master of language who expresses human truth—truth, as Keats puts it, "felt upon the pulses"—the truth of feeling, of thought, of action, of imagination, of aspiration, which we ordinary folk can only articulate vaguely, clumsily, fumblingly, in a way that actualizes all the potentialities of speech: melody, rhythm, imagery, meaning. This is art, but it is also prophecy in the etymological meaning of the word:

sound-structure of its sentences." (René Wellek and Austin Warren, *Theory of Literature* [New York: Harcourt, Brace, 1949], p. 157.)

prophanein—to bring forth to light, to manifest, to declare—*declarare,* that is, to make clear. Thus the poet is, in an analogical sense, a creator: he brings into existence a world of ordered and radiant speech, an integrated, harmonious, effulgent world of language which, though it is, considered from the aspect of its matter, nothing more than a series of sounds heard or imagined, is yet able to enrich our lives extraordinarily. "A nothing," if you will, and yet, in the words of a contemporary philosopher, "a wonderful world in itself, which, through its concretizations in our consciousness, calls forth deep transformations in our lives, widens these lives and elevates them above the flats and levels of daily existence, endows them [at times] with a divine splendor."[91]

[91] *Das Literarische Kunstwerk,* p. 389. The present writer has prepared a paraphrase and discussion of Ingarden's book in a study to be published as part of a volume by the Georgetown University Press, Washington, D.C.

Poetry has been doing this for a long time, and it will continue to do so, in spite of the positivist's contempt and the obscurantist's rhapsodic adulation.

The Aquinas Lectures

Published by the Marquette University Press,
Milwaukee 3, Wisconsin

St. Thomas and the Life of Learning (1937) by
the late Fr. John F. McCormick, S.J., professor of philosophy, Loyola University.

St. Thomas and the Gentiles (1938) by Morti-
mer J. Adler, Ph.D., director of the Institute
of Philosophical Research, San Francisco,
Calif.

St. Thomas and the Greeks (1939) by Anton C.
Pegis, Ph.D., former president and present
professor of the Pontifical Institute of Mediaeval Studies, Toronto.

The Nature and Functions of Authority (1940)
by Yves Simon, Ph.D., professor of philosophy of social thought, University of Chicago.

St. Thomas and Analogy (1941) by Fr. Gerald
B. Phelan, Ph.D., professor of philosophy, St.
Michael's College, Toronto.

St. Thomas and the Problem of Evil (1942) by
Jacques Maritain, Ph.D., professor *emeritus*
of philosophy, Princeton University.

Humanism and Theology (1943) by Werner Jaeger, Ph.D., Litt.D., University professor, Harvard University.

The Nature and Origins of Scientism (1944) by John Wellmuth.

Cicero in the Courtroom of St. Thomas Aquinas (1945) by the late E. K. Rand, Ph.D., Litt.D., LL.D., Pope professor of Latin, *emeritus*, Harvard University.

St. Thomas and Epistemology (1946) by Fr. Louis-Marie Regis, O.P., Th.L., Ph.D., director of the Albert the Great Institute of Mediaeval Studies, University of Montreal.

St. Thomas and the Greek Moralists (1947, Spring) by Vernon J. Bourke, Ph.D., professor of philosophy, St. Louis University, St. Louis, Missouri.

History of Philosophy and Philosophical Education (1947, Fall) by Étienne Gilson of the *Académie française*, director of studies and professor of the history of Mediaeval philosophy, Pontifical Institute of Mediaeval Studies, Toronto.

The Natural Desire for God (1948) by Fr. William R. O'Connor, S.T.L., Ph.D., former professor of dogmatic theology, St. Joseph's Seminary, Dunwoodie, N.Y.

St. Thomas and the World State (1949) by Robert M. Hutchins, former Chancellor of the University of Chicago.

Method in Metaphysics (1950) by Fr. Robert J. Henle, S.J., dean of the graduate school, St. Louis University, St. Louis, Missouri.

Wisdom and Love in St. Thomas Aquinas (1951) by Étienne Gilson of the *Académie française,* director of studies and professor of the history of Mediaeval philosophy, Pontifical Institute of Mediaeval Studies, Toronto.

The Good in Existential Metaphysics (1952) by Elizabeth G. Salmon, associate professor of philosophy in the graduate school, Fordham University.

St. Thomas and the Object of Geometry (1953) by Vincent Edward Smith, Ph.D., professor of philosophy, University of Notre Dame.

Realism and Nominalism Revisited (1954) by Henry Veatch, Ph.D., professor of philosophy, Indiana University.

Imprudence in St. Thomas Aquinas (1955) by Charles J. O'Neil, Ph.D., professor of philosophy, Marquette University.

The Truth That Frees (1956) by Fr. Gerard Smith, S.J., Ph.D., professor and chairman of the department of philosophy, Marquette University.

St. Thomas and the Future of Metaphysics (1957) by Fr. Joseph Owens, C.Ss.R., associate professor of philosophy, Pontifical Institute of Mediaeval Studies, Toronto.

Thomas and the Physics of 1958: A Confrontation (1958) by Henry Margenau, Ph.D., Eugene Higgins professor of physics and natural philosophy, Yale University.

Metaphysics and Ideology (1959) by Wm. Oliver Martin, professor of philosophy, University of Rhode Island.

Language, Truth and Poetry (1960) by Victor M. Hamm, Ph.D., Professor of English, Marquette University.

Uniform format, cover and binding.